Marketing Quiz

Business Culture – MCQs – Case Studies

Claude LAVEINE

Certaines informations de ce livre sont purement anecdotiques et imaginaires. Toute ressemblance avec une personne physique ou morale existante ou ayant existé est purement fortuite.

This book is a work of fiction. Any resemblance to a natural or legal person, existing or having existed is purely coincidental. The anecdotes and information cited are the fruit of the author's imagination.

Copyright©2020 Claude LAVEINE
Tous droits réservés.
ISBN-13 : 9798553915995

From the same author

La Vie Epatante de l'Agent Secret Duchemin – Tome 1
Il Faut Sauver l'Agent Secret Duchemin – Tome 2
Agent Secret Duchemin – Mission Lune – Tome 3
Au Temps en Emporte l'Agent Duchemin – Tome 4
Le Fabuleux Destin de l'Agent Duchemin – Tome 5
Agent Secret Duchemin-En Avant Mars – Tome 6
Agent Secret Duchemin – A Mars Forcée – Tome 7
Agent Secret Duchemin - Un Héros Français -Tome 8
Agent Secret Duchemin-Opération Rédemption-Tome 9

L'Effarante Aventure de Brian Tabernak – Tome 1
L'Incroyable Attaque de l'agent Tabernak - Tome 2
La Terrible Traque de l'Equipe Tabernak – Tome 3
L'Equipe Tabernak Contre-Attaque – Tome 4
Des Agents pas très Secrets – Opération Esturgeon
Des Agents pas très Secrets – Mission Caméléon
Des Agents pas très Secrets - Maudite Météorite

Constantin Dumoulin – Panique sous les Tropiques
Constantin Dumoulin – Branle-Bas de Combat aux USA
Constantin Dumoulin – Secret Fatal au Lac Baïkal
Robin Dubois – Sans Froid ni Loi – Tome 1
Robin Dubois – Espion malgré moi – Tome 2

The Exciting Life of Secret Agent Duchemin – Volume 1
The Amazing Adventure of Brian Tabernak – Volume 1
The Incredible Attack of Agent Tabernak – Volume 2

Quiz de Marketing-Tome 1
Quiz de Marketing-Tome 2
Quiz de Marketing International
Quiz de Management Commercial
Marketing Quiz

Marketing Calculations

Contents

From the same author 4
How to use this book ? 8
A/ Marketing Culture 10
B/ Marketing Key Points 19
C/ Marketing Calculations 27
D/ Marketing Principles 35
E/ Advertising Culture 45
F/ Marketing MCQs 52
G/ Case Studies 59
H/ Economic Culture 68
I/ International Marketing Calculations 79
J/ International Negotiation 85
K/ Geography Quiz 90
From the same author 97

How to use this book ?

This book allows you to prepare your exams or diplomas and to improve your business culture. To optimize reading, we recommend that the reader uses a paper notepad and a calculator.

Answers to marketing culture questions and calculations are presented regularly. Answers are numbered and often corrected on the same page.

If you are looking for more calculations, we recommend "Marketing Calculations" by the same author in the Kindle store. For more information in International Trade, we recommend "Quiz de Marketing International" by the same author. This book will be regularly updated on the Kindle store. It is dated January 2023.

Some informations are purely anecdotal and imaginary. Any resemblance to a physical or legal person existing or having existed is purely coincidental.

A/ Marketing Culture

True or False

1) By 2035, the world population will increase by 15% to 8.5 billion people and consume 30% more food, 45% more water and 55% more energy than today:
2) France's first commercial partner is the United States:
3) China is France's second supplier, France is China's 20th supplier:
4) The number of trainees in France has been divided by two in 5 years:
5) In Singapore, 1 in 6 households is a millionaire in US dollars:
6) 26% of Russian men do not reach the age of 55:
7) 1% of Americans have benefited from 90% of income increases for the 5 past years:

1) True, 2) False, Germany, 3) True, 4) False, has been doubled, 5) True, 6) True, 7) True.

8) Knowing that the advertising costs are included in the selling price, on average a family pays each month without knowing it: € 133 for advertising - € 153 - € 143.
9) The selling price of a car sold in France includes on average: € 1,200 in advertising costs –
€ 1,400 - € 1,700.
10) What does the Internet mean?

8) 153 €, 9) 1200 €, 10) International Network.

1) What is the favorite destination of French people going abroad?

12) What is the most consumed drink in France after drinking water? True or False

13) 90% of new products disappear six months after their commercial launch:

14) Marketing expenses for a new consumer product often reach 8 to 10 million euros:

15) In order to reassure their passengers, some airlines perfume their planes with the smell of honey and breast milk:

16) Some car manufacturers study the noise of the doors to give a feeling of robustness:

17) In Quebec, cola sodas are nicknamed "moose juice in furious water":

11) Spain, 12) Mineral water, 13) True, 14) True, 15) True, 16) True, 17) True.

18) Certain advertisements for sodas were produced in the American space shuttle:

19) To attract customers, a New York restaurant employs only twin waiters:

20) Every second 100,000 bottles of cola soda are consumed on the planet:

18) True, 19) True, 20) True.

♦♦♦

21) In French couples, what percentage of women are involved in shopping, washing and ironing?
22) What is the average rental cost per m2 on the Champs Elysées of a sales area on the right side going up towards the Arc de Triomphe?
23) What is the most spoken language in the world?
24) What is the number of countries where English is the official language: 70 - 47 - 28
25) What is the number of countries where French is the official language:

21) Shopping (90%), laundry (95%), ironing (97%), 22) € 9,000 per year, 23) The Mandarin, 24) 47, 25) 30.

♦♦♦

Did you know it ?

1) What are the losses of a retail point due to theft, lost and damaged products?
2) On average, what is the percentage of losses in relation to turnover?
3) What is the average weight of a shopping cart when it arrives at the checkout: 19 kg - 28 kg - 30 kg?
4) What is the average purchase for a hypermarket customer: € 53 - € 72 - € 90?
5) What is the average number of visits by a French person to a hypermarket in a year: 47 - 51 - 38?

6) What is the average time spent by a customer in a hypermarket: 35 min - 40 min - 1 h 30?

1) Unknown markdown, 2) About 5%, 3) 30 kg, 4) 72 €, 5) 38, 6) 40 minutes.

7) Among the five senses, which is the finest and which has the most memory?
8) What is the average monthly cost to perfume 100 m2 of sales area?

7) Sense of smell, 8) 70 €.

True or False

1) The first tests of artificial perfume in a retail point took place in American department stores in 1922:
2) Wild rose and jasmine are the flowers most used to perfume retail points:
3) Perfuming a retail point can create an atmosphere, contain tensions and make you want to stay longer:
4) Soothing odors can multiply a turnover by three:
5) Perfuming fruits and vegetables is allowed:

1) True, 2) True, 3) True, 4) True, 5) False, misleading advertising.

6) 70% of the choice of products in a retail point is made in front of the shelves:
7) Some billboards also spread attractive odors:
8) With geomarketing, it is possible to know the consumption potential , district by district in a big city, for more than 900 products:
9) Geomarketing makes it possible to calculate the amount of the entry fee of a franchise:
10) Some stores have created their own radio channel:

6) True, 7) True, 8) True, 9) True, 10) True.

11) A hypermarket offers around 20,000 references:
12) A supermarket makes an average of € 7,000 per m2:
13) Chinese hypermarkets sell live fish:

11) False, more than 50,000, 12) False, around € 4,000, 13) True.

True or False

1) France represents 1% of the human population, 4% of the planet's GDP and 16% of global social spending:
2) The United States has 1,600 millionaires more than last year, the United Kingdom 460, France 300 and Germany 230:
3) On the stock market, the number one company in social networks is estimated at 200 billion dollars, the number

one in sodas at 190 billion and the number one in IT at 180 billion:
4) 90 % of American families are richer than they were in 1985:
5) The number one threat to humanity? Inequalities for the French, nuclear power for the Japanese, disease for the Chinese:
6) 280,000 French people study abroad, 60,000 foreigners study in France:

1) True, 2) True, 3) True, 4) False, 5) True, 6) False, the reverse.

7) Which 5 countries receive the most tourists in millions in descending order?
8) What are the top 5 countries in terms of tourism revenue in billions of euros in descending order?
9) What is the average cost of a 30-second advertising spot just before the evening news in France?
10) What are the top 3 European countries in terms of attracting foreign industrial investment in descending order?

7) France (85), USA (68), China (59), Spain (58), Italy (46) 8) USA (100), Spain (45), France (43), China (40), Macao (35), 9) € 45,000, 10) United Kingdom, Germany, France.

11) The average annual compensation of CEOs of large IT groups has been $ 60 million over the past 5 years:

12) The Austrians take 36 days of paid vacation per year, the Greeks 35, the French 34, the Italians 30 and Germans 28:

13) The French consume 150 million cigarettes, 32 million baguettes and 300,000 jars of jam every day:

14) Women produce 60% of the world's work and 45% of the food, but only receive 10% of revenues:

15) Out of 60 million toys bought in France each year, 35 million are thrown away after 6 months:

11) True, 12) True, 13) True, 14) True, 15) True.

15) What does the iSleep application, one of the most downloaded by young European executives, offer?

16) Which European country has the highest productivity per employee?

17) After Ireland, which European country has the highest fertility rate?

18) Which European country has a lifespan for men of 78 years and for women of 85 years? 19) What is the average margin rate of an application sold on an electronic platform?

15) During the nap, noises of keyboard, stapler and drawers, 16) France, 17) France, 18) France, 19) 70%.

◆◆◆

1) The « Grands Magasins » district in Paris attracts 45 million visitors each year, including 16 million tourists:
2) The richest 10% of French people hold 45% of the national wealth:
3) One in two French people is subject to the property tax:
4) France is the world's leading exporting country in terms of turnover:
5) French people spend around 30 hours a month on the internet:
6) Tourism in France has generated 80 billion euros last year:
1) True, 2) True, 3) False, 1 in 100, 4) False, Germany, 5) True, 6) True.

◆◆◆

7) 80% of suppliers of electronic components are located in China:
8) In the European Union, a woman must work 60 days more than a man to earn the same salary:
7) True, 8) True.

B/ Marketing Key Points

1) What are the five classic stages of the life cycle of a product or a service?
2) What are the characteristics of the maturity phase?
3) What are the characteristics of the launch phase?
4) What elements of the marketing plan or Mix can be modified to relaunch a product?
5) How to name the 6 particular life curves?
6) What are the functions of the brand?
7) What are the essential characteristics of a good brand?
8) A trade mark may not:
9) What are the different types of brand?

1) Research, launch, growth, maturity, decline,
2) Break-even point exceeded, full profitability, stable demand, reconstituted cash flow, customer loyalty,
3) High costs, random profitability, stock creation,
4) Packaging, price, content, advertising,
5) Imperialist products (sodas), fashion products, residual market (skateboard), dilemma product, immediate success, ephemeral product (music market),
6) Conveying an image, a style - guaranteeing the product quality, securing the consumer, standing out from the competition,
7) Memorable, readable, evocative, translatable, declinable, euphonic (harmonious sound),
8) Harming others, being generic (The Butter), misleading,
9) Product, "umbrella", signature, distribution, notorious.

◆◆◆

10) With which organizations can a trademark be protected?

11) Can a company use an already registered trademark?

12) What are the consequences of counterfeiting for a brand?

13) How to define the image of a brand?

14) What are the functions of packaging?

15) How to improve the functional quality of a product?

16) How to improve the aesthetic quality of a product?

17) What are the 3 main standards for France, Europe and the World?

18) Name 4 quality labels?

19) What are the 3 types of new product?

10) National Institute of Industrial Property (INPI, Paris), Office for Harmonization of the Internal Market (OHMI, Alicante), World Organization of Industrial Property (OMPI, Geneva),

11) Yes, if the sector activity is different, in the event of negotiation, in the event of purchase or rental (franchise),

12) Loss of turnover, threat to the brand image, legal costs, disorganization of the sales network,

13) Affective and rational representation associated with a name,

14) Protection against external aggressions, transport, handling, implementation in the store, communication in the retail point,

15) Security, modernity, ease of use, efficiency,

16) Design and style ,

17) NF (French standards, Afnor), CE (European Community), ISO (International Standard Organization, ONU),
18) Red label, AOC (Designation of origin controlled), AB (organic farming), Atout qualité,
19) Discontinuity (Digital Sound), semi-continuity (DVD), continuity (flat screen).

21) What are the 5 types of market?
22) Who are the 5 main actors in a market?
23) What are the 4 main environments of the corporate market?
24) What does "hourglass effect" mean?
25) What are the 5 needs evoked by Maslow in a pyramid?
26) What are the 3 types of motivation?
27) What are the 2 elements that constitute the purchasing obstacles?
28) What are the 3 types of attitudes?

21) Atomized (multitude of offerers), open (websites), closed (car market), current, potential,
22) Consumers, producers, prescribers (do not buy but recommend to buy), advisers, distributors,
23) Technological, legal, socio-economic, cultural,
24) Widening of the high-end and low-end segments, over-segmentation of the offer,
25) Physiological, security, social, esteem, fulfillment,

26) Hedonistic (self satisfaction), oblative (generosity), self-expression (need for recognition),
27) Fears and inhibitions,
28) Cognitive (knowledge of the product), affective (sympathy with the brand), conative (triggering the purchase).

30) What are the 4 Ps of the Marketing Mix:
31) What are the 5 elements of the marketing plan:
32) What is the translation of the following terms: .Mix, Merchandising, Packaging, Marketing, Design, Market test, Benchmarking, Cash , Phoning, Mailing, Show room:
33) What do Operational Marketing, Social Marketing, Political Marketing, Sensory Marketing mean:
34) What is the vocation of consumerism:
35) What do UFC, INC, DGCCRF, CNC mean:
36) What are the forms of action of consumer associations:

30) Product, price, place, promotion (advertising, sales force),
31) Product, price, distribution, sales force, communication,
32) None, they are used in english all over the world.
33) Application of 4P to launch a new product, commercial techniques applied to the development of charitable associations, commercial promotion of political parties, use of the five senses to attract the attention of consumers,
34) Defend, protect and alert consumers,
35) Federal Union of Consumers, National Institute of Consumer Affairs, Directorate General for Consumer Affairs,

Competition and Fraud Prevention, National Council for competition,

36) Influence purchasing behavior, put pressure on public authorities, boycott, legal actions.

37) Cite 4 probabilistic methods to determine a sample of consumers:

38) What do they mean: Quota method, Itinerary method:

39) Cite 5 types of questions used in a market research questionnaire:

40) Cite 2 methods to sort the results of a survey:

41) What does "consumer panel" mean:

42) What are 4 advantages of segmentation:

43) Cite 4 relevant, measurable and operational criteria to segment a market:

44) How to calculate a Market Share in volume and value:

37) Successive random draw, in clusters, systematic, random number tables,

38) Reduced model of the base population, choice of route to administer a questionnaire,

39) Closed, open, mcq, with classification, filter,

40) Flat, cross-sorted,

41) Permanent representative sample of a population,

42) Adapt the Marketing Mix, target and make profitable advertising communication, build customer loyalty, optimize geomarketing,

43) Demographic, geographic, socio-economic, psychological,

44) Quantities sold of the company / Quantities sold of the market, Turnover of the company / Turnover of the market.

45) 8 constraints to determine a selling price:

46) Meaning of: round price, magic price, minimum price, maximum price, recommended price:

47) 8 reasons to modify a selling price:

48) 5 legal constraints in terms of price:

49) Criteria for allocating space in supermarkets:

50) 3 reasons to reference a product in a point of sale:

51) Why sell services in supermarkets:

52) 3 dimensions of the assortment:

45) Costs (fixed, variable, break-even point), product type, level of range, margin rate, demand, competition, distribution method, commercial strategy (alignment, skimming, penetration),

46) Ends with one or several zero, just below the rounded price, linked to insufficient quality (psychological price), linked to excessive price (psychological price), recommended by the supplier,

47) Quantities sold, level of range, payment date, delivery time, discounts, rebates, price cut, date of purchase (yield management, adjustment of the price in real time depending on the offer and demand),

48) Sale at a loss, agreements, unmarked price, old unmarked price if discounts, misleading advertising,

49) Product turnover rate, occupied space, attractiveness index, sensitivity to turnover and gross profit index,

50) Central purchasing office, margin rate, novelty, negotiations with suppliers,

51) Diversifying the offer and be less dependent on the sale of food products, attracting customers by competitive prices, competing with independent traders and websites,

52) Depth (multiple references for the same brand), width (multiple families of products), length (total number of references).

C/ Marketing Calculations

A) 28% of motorists who already have a car radio would like a more efficient one. 5% of motorists do not have a car radio. Among them, 45% plan to buy one. 35% of motorists install their car radio themselves. 7 million passenger vehicles are in circulation. What is the potential market for motorists who want a car radio installed by a professional?

A) *Answers:*
Motorists without radio: 7,000,000 x 5% x 45% = 157,500 motorists who plan to buy one, Motorists with radio: 7,000,000 x 95% x 28% = 1,862,000 motorists who would like to change of car radio, (95% = 100% - 5%) 157,500 + 1,862,000 = 2,019,500 x 65%
(100% - 35%) = 1,312,675 motorists would buy a car radio and have it installed.

B) The Chocod'or company must plan its advertising budget for the next two years. Due to competition, the N + 1 and N + 2 turnovers are expected to decrease by 7%. In year N, the advertising budget represented around 4.06% of the turnover.

In order to limit expenses, Chocod'or wishes to return to budgets of around 2.5%.

Turnover in year N: 100 million euros.

What will be the amounts of advertising budgets in N and N + 1?

B) *Answers:*
Turnover N + 1: 93,000,000 (100,000,000 - 7%),
Turnover N + 2: 86,490,000 (93,000,000 - 7%)
Advertising budget year N: 4,060,000 (100,000,000 x 4.06%),
Advertising budget for year N + 1: 2,325,000 (93,000,000 x 2.5%).

C) What is the price excluding taxes of the following products:
The h.t price is calculated by dividing the t.t.c price by 100% + the % of VAT. VAT = 20%,
the h.t will be calculated by doing: t.t.c / 1.20. (h.t price: price without taxes, t.t.c price: price including taxes).
Selling prices including VAT (20% VAT):
.Large screen TV set: € 890,
.SUV Luxury: € 39,000,
. Round trip Paris London on Fly Away: € 99,
.One night at Motel GoodNight: € 59,
.A Tiptop smartphone: € 690:

C) *Answers:*

.TV h.t: € 741,66, SUV h.t: € 32,500, Fly Away h.t: € 82,5, Motel h.t: € 49,16, Smartphone h.t: € 575. The prices are entered before tax by a company. VAT is collected on sales and

deducted on purchases. The balance of VAT is paid quarterly to the tax authorities.

D / A manufacturer of nylon ropes has produced during the last 5 years:
N: 2,000,000 meters, N + 1: 2,400,000 meters, N + 2: 2,600,000 meters, N + 3: 2,700,000 meters , N + 4: 2,800,000 meters.
The share of ropes exported was in:
N / 800,000 meters, N + 1: 840,000, N + 2: 860,000, N + 3: 900,000, N + 4: 920,000.
What is the evolution rate between each year (T1 - T0 / T0 x 100)?
What is the average evolution rate from N to N + 4?
What is the exports share in percentage for each year?

D/ *Answers:*

N + 1: 20%, N + 2: 8.3%, N + 3: 3.8%, N + 4: 3.7%, over 4 years: 8.95%, N: 40 %, N + 1: 35%, N + 2: 33.07%, N + 3: 33.33%, N + 4: 32.85%.

E) Amanda Ltd is the leader in roasted almonds in France, distributed in large and medium-sized stores.
French population in mainland France: 64,000,000 inhabitants, Distribution of the French population:

Under 15 years: 25% (10% almond consumers), 15/65 years: 62% (80% almond consumers), Over 65: 13% (85% almond consumers).

French consumption of almonds: 250,000 tons, 75% of French people are likely to consume almonds.

In year N, Amanda Ltd sold 75,000 tons of almonds in France.

Calculate the theoretical market, the potential market and the real market in France for roasted almonds.

What is Amanda's real market share?

E) *Answers:*

Theoretical market: 64,000,000 consumers,
Potential market: 48,000,000 consumers (64,000,000 x 75%),
Real market: (64,000,000 x 25% x 10%) + (64,000,000 x 62% x 80%) + (64,000,000 x 13% x 85%) = 40,416,000 consumers, (1,600,000 + 31,744,000 + 7,072,000),
Amanda's real market share: 75,000/250,000 tons x 100: 30%.

F) From the following calculation formulas, calculate the profitability of the two brands studied in supermarkets:

.Gross margin = Sales price excluding taxes - Purchase price excluding taxes,

.Brand rates = Gross margin / Sales prices without taxes x 100,

. Multiplier coefficient = Sales price ttc / Purchase price ht (ttc: VAT included, ht: without VAT),

.Gross profit = Gross margin x Quantities sold, .Average stock = Initial stock + Final stock / 2, .Turnover coefficient = Sold quantities / Average stock,

.Shelves attractiveness index = Purchasing index / Passage index

.Sensitivity index compared to Turnover = % Turnover / % LD,

(LD = Linear developed, linear on the ground in meters multiplied by the number of levels), .Sensitivity index compared to Gross Profit = % GP / % LD,

.After calculating the sensitivity indexes, if the results are greater than 1: the product is under represented, we must increase its space in the linear ; if the results are less than 1, the product is over represented, we must reduce its space in the linear .

1 or 100% is the average for the product family.

You are responsible for the Scented Candles department at your point of sale.

You want to compare the profitability of "Smell +" and "TopFlavor".

"Smell +": Purchase price ht: € 14, Sale price ht: € 29, Quantities sold: 26,000, LD: 8 meters, AS: 3,200.

"TopFlavor": Purchase price ht: € 17, Sale price ht : € 26, Quantities sold: 23,000, LD: 6 meters, AS: 1,600.

Calculate the gross margin, the brand rate, the gross profit, the turnover coefficient, the profitability of the shelf space, the profitability index.

F) *Answers:*

"*Smell +*": Gross margin(GM): 29 - 14 = € 15, Brand rate(BR): 15/29 x 100 = 51.72%, Gross Profit(GP): 15 x 26,000 = € 390,000, Rotation Rate(RR): 26,000 / 3,200 = 8.12, the stock is renewed more than 8 times over the period studied, Shelf Profitability(SP): GP / LD: 390,000 / 8 = € 48,750 per linear meter, Profitability Index(PI): SP x RR / 1000: 48,750 x 8.12 / 1000 = 395.8.

"*TopFlavor*": GM: € 9, BR: 34.61%, GP: € 207,000, RR: 14.37, SP: € 34,500 per linear meter, PI: 495.7. Taking into account the RR, SP and L.D, the space allocated in the shelf to "*TopFlavor*" should be increased.

G) From the following formulas, calculate the break-even point:

.Break-even point in volume (Quantities): Fixed Costs / Unit Contribution Margin,

.Unit Contribution Margin : Unit sale price - Unit variable cost,

.Break-even point in value (Euros): Fixed Costs x Turnover / Contribution Margin, .Contribution Margin: Turnover - Variable Costs, .Financial result: Contribution Margin - Fixed Costs,

.Break-even date: Break-even point in value x 360 / Turnover,

.Differential analysis: Turnover - Variable Costs = Contribution Margin - Fixed Costs = Result (Loss or Profit)

.Variable costs depend on the evolution of turnover (sales premiums, raw materials),
.Fixed costs do not depend on turnover and are paid even if the company does not sell any product, (rental, energy, wages).

PlaySoft wants to market a new video game at € 390. The variable unit cost is € 210. Fixed costs amount to € 700,000.
Sales are estimated at 80,000 units.
1) What is the break-even point in volume and value?
2) If the unit cost increases by 26%, what should be the selling price of the video game?
3) What will be the financial result if 80,000 units are sold?
4) What will be the net result after tax (36% of taxation)?

1) Break even point in volume : 700,000/180 = 3,889 packs approximately. At this level of sales, the company makes neither loss nor profit.
Break even point in value: 3889 packs x 390 = € 1,516,710. If using the formula: T x FC / CM, 31,200,000 x 700,000 / 14,400,000 = € 1,516,666. The slight difference in result is normal and results from rounding up the figures.
2) Knowing that an increase in costs causes an increase in the sale price in the same proportion: 390 x 1.26 = € 491.4
3) Without change in sales price and variable cost,
T: 31,200,000 (390 x 80,000),
VC: 16,800,000 (210 x 80,000),
CM:14,400,000 (180 x 80,000)
FC: 700,000,
R: € 13,700,000 (Profit).

4) 13,700,000 x 0.64 (100 - 36) = € 8,768,000.

D/ Marketing Principles

Marketing is the art of selling to the consumer what they want to buy. Many companies therefore spend fortunes on market research, research and development, communication and sales force in order to impose their innovations. As the failure rate for new products is high, some marketing departments are trying to revert to less expensive methods that are more respectful of sustainable development.

Marketing books often teach that you have to flatter the customer, their ego and manipulate their innate need for recognition. The statutory purchase or the snob effect are marketing classics. I buy, therefore I am. All luxury goods use this method. The margins are comfortable and the customer is satisfied. The Maslow pyramid, socio styles and market research are aimed at understanding the reasons for purchasing by ever more volatile and unfaithful consumers. Lack of time, electronic platforms, the infinite choice offered by the internet make the customer ever more demanding and inconstant.
Never have customers had so many choices.

Marketing therefore seems essential. But confusing trade and short-term profit does not allow the sustainability of a company and its range of products / services. Many companies have taken years to capitalize on new products in order to acquire satisfied and loyal customers. The often maligned Marketing is not a magic solution to sell. These are coordinated actions, organized and measured according to the time and the type of client.

In a free market with strong competition, Marketing often allows companies to survive and develop. Marketing abuse can also stifle a market. The difficulty of a marketing department is therefore to find a subtle balance between the need to sell, to resist competitors, to launch new products and to communicate with authenticity.

Studying the market can include lavish spending. The participation of panelists, investigators, psychologists helps to better understand consumer expectations. Techniques based on chance or reproduction in a sample of the mother population have proven their worth. But this determination to always study everything can also lead to sudden and unexpected changes in behavior. The current example is streaming entertainment. The big television channels have widely used and abused advertising and have formatted a number of programs according to the expectations of viewers.

The result is that many households now either refuse conventional television or watch it much less. Streaming has eliminated advertising. Video on demand eliminated the imposed and limited choice of programs. Freedom of choice won. The spectator can no longer be considered as a passive actor who ingests advertisements without thinking. Those days are over.

The Internet and its multiple sites or platforms are also empowering customers. One click and he changes supplier. This multiplicity of offers changes the attitude of customers. Abusing internet advertising again is a classic reflex that will lead to the same effects.

Some companies are even now refusing to advertise. Their principle is to base their entire strategy on the quality of the service provided, the welcome at the point of sale and positive word of mouth.

Even if it may be obvious, the quality of the customer's welcome at the point of sale is decisive, and sometimes forgotten. Some managers of service companies also believe that it is better to first train, motivate and properly supervise their teams rather than spending astronomical sums on advertising.

Large service groups have sometimes discovered belatedly that spending millions of euros on advertising has limited effects if staff do not feel concerned and recognized.

Investing in human capital is often much more effective.

All Management techniques inspired by Organizational Behavior aim to improve the development of employees. If my employee is satisfied with his activity, the client will realize this and my sales will increase. Basic but often very effective reasoning.

Start by believing in your employees, trust them, give them the means to learn and understand allows you to limit Marketing budgets that are ever more extensible.

Management and Marketing are linked. Selling without mastering the commercial methods is long and difficult. But selling with convinced and concerned staff is even better.

Selling a product without a seller and without communication is often complicated and perilous, but many companies have chosen quality and managed to convince over the long term.

The most difficult thing is not to sell once but to repeat the sale. Getting the customer back is a complex process. The quality of sales staff is vital. Sales professions are sometimes overlooked, but how to do Marketing without having sold anything.

Marketing remains the art of selling. All the artifices which surround the trade and its multiple strategies are often an attractive decor but nothing can replace a good salesman.

The crux of the war is turnover and above all the operating margin. Marketing by selling off your products is a short-term solution. Recruiting effective salespeople has always been tricky, but current changes and new technologies show the urgency of trusting its sellers. Learning to express yourself correctly, to argue, to show great tenacity, to innovate are assets for all professions in a company.

Selling leads to Marketing. Marketing leads to the customer. Like all sciences, Marketing is essential but is not a magic potion. Learning to master the techniques is very useful for developing your commercial activity, but abusing it sometimes leads to rapid decline. Marketing is primarily about selling. Nothing prevents us from respecting our employees, respecting our customers and doing business with quality products and efficient service.

The purpose of this book is to help you memorize all of these sales techniques. Long live Marketing.

Market Study

A company cannot launch a product/service without a market study. The marketing concept is to sell products/services our consumers want to buy. We can create a product/service and then try to sell it, but frequently it will be difficult to find buyers. Because of hard competition, in a free market, we have to use the marketing techniques.

If we want to find customers, we need to ask them : what do you want to buy and why ? Most of the time, a market study is based on interviews with test customers.

We ask them many questions about the competition, the market and their feelings. Most of them are selected at random or because they represent an accurate type of customer. We also need to analyse the main figures of our market, the turnover estimate, the potential expenditures, the budget.

Break Even Point

The break even point can be determined in volume (products sold) and in turnover ($, €). Especially for a new company, it is essential to estimate this break even point. We need to know when we are able to cover our full costs (Variable and Fixed costs). The first cent of profit will be essential for the company. At the break even point, we have no profit, no loss. A company cannot survive without any profit. We need to innovate, to create new product/services and to recruit new employees and executives. On average, we lose almost 10% of our customers each year, for multiple reasons. Some of our products/services decline because of new technologies and new competitors. The break even point helps us to determine the B.E.P date and the volume/turnover estimate. These figures are necessary to prepare a budget, to plan the sales objectives and the commissions of the salespeople. Il will also help the company in planning the costs. The variable costs depend on the turnover, the more we sell, the more we must pay our salespeople (commissions, bonuses). The fixed costs do not change, whatever the turnover. Even if we do not sell anything, we must pay the office rental, electricity, heating.

Psychological Price

The main issue for a company is to find the right price, for the right product/service at the right time. First of all, we must take into account our total costs in order to keep a minimum profit margin. This profit margin will enable to launch new products/services, to invest in the workforce, to innovate and to increase our turnover. Most of the time we can sell at a higher price, at a lower price or at the same price than our competitors. Therefore, we have to analyse their pricing strategy and try to adapt to the market.

At the end of the process, we may use a Psychological Price study by interviewing test consumers regarding their feeling of the product/service. According to their knowledge of the market and the competitors, they will give their opinion about the quality of the product/service and about the final price. These exercises are able to give an estimate of the right price, according to the customers knowledge. The final price, after all our market studies (total costs, competitors price, psychological price), will be a magical price. Always a few cents under the full price. For example, 9.99 cents.

Surprisingly, whatever the product/service and the country, even one cent under the full price will enable to sell more than the full price, 10 cents. One of the mysteries of marketing. Finally, the psychological price is a good summary of the marketing concept, how to adapt to the consumers and sell at the price they are looking for. And not the contrary.

Advertising

Advertising is an essential activity in Marketing. However many consumers think that they are saturated with advertising messages. Many people do not watch T.V channels anymore mainly because they are fed up with advertising. The recent success of streaming T.V channels and video on demand is the answer of disappointed consumers. Advertising prices are always higher and represent a big amount of money for a company. If we decide to advertise on the internet or in classical media, we must be sure of the final target and audience. According to the very high costs of advertising, we have to select correctly the final reader, watcher or listener of the ad.

We must also be sure that we have an advertising budget and a correct media plan. Our product/service must be seen or watched in the right media at the right time. Some companies do not spend any money in advertising and use only word of mouth advices or social media. It can be efficient too.

Sales Management

Sales management is one of the most difficult tasks of a company. Even an excellent product/service will be hard to sell without salespeople.

These salespeople are more and more difficult to recruit. Most of the Business Schools students dream of marketing jobs and do not want to sell anything. Surprisingly, marketing is first of all the art of selling, but for many people it is associated to strategy and advertising.

It would be strange to become a brand manager without a selling experience first. Therefore, the salespeople need to be very well motivated. All the commissions and bonuses have already been invented and must be calculated correctly. But, maybe the most important, salespeople need to feel good in the company. Selling everyday is a hard job with many disappointing moments.

The sales objectives are more and more ambitious and the competitors are always more agressive. That is why we need to calculate very precisely the motivation plans, the sales budget, the sales unit and salespeople efficiency.

If you need more informations about the calculations, we recommend you "Marketing Calculations", from the same author on the Kindle Store.

E/ Advertising Culture

Did you know it ?

1) Classify from one to eleven in descending order of advertising investment these different communication techniques: Event advertising, professional directories, direct marketing, television, press, sales promotion, public relations, posters, radio, internet, cinema.

1) Event advertising (5), professional directories (8), direct marketing (1), television (4), press (3), sales promotion (2), public relations (6), posters (7), radio (9), internet (10), cinema (11).

2) From the following initials, find the different Direct Marketing techniques:
D.M, T, M, e.M, V.M, B.M, T.F, TF.N, A.N, I.N, SMS, MMS.

2) Direct mail, telephone, mailing, e.mailing, video mailing, bus mailing (group mailing), trade fair, toll-free number, azure number, indigo number, short message system, multi media system.

3) What is the ranking of the six main media in descending order in advertising investment?

45

3) Press, television, posters, radio, internet, cinema.

4) Which are the competitors who are driving down the audience of conventional television channels?

4) Video on demand, video streaming platform, internet, digital TV channels.

5) Find the communication media to which the following advertising costs correspond: (Average price per medium for a passage, on the radio: 15-second spot, on television: 30-second spot)

€ 15,000 for a four-color page,

€ 22,000 for a four-color page,

€ 4,500 for 15 seconds,

€ 45,000 for 30 seconds,

€ 105,000 for 30 seconds,

€ 3,200 for 4 x 3 for 7 days in Paris,

$ 3 million for 30 seconds.

5) € 15,000 for a full color page (Press Magazine),

€ 22,000 for a full color page (Daily Press),

€ 4,500 for 15 seconds (Radio),

€ 45,000 for 30 seconds (French TV),

€ 105,000 for 30 seconds (American television),

€ 3,200 for 4 x 3 for 7 days in Paris (Billboard),

$ 3 million for 30 seconds (SuperBowl in the USA).

A four-color page is the printer format for a color page with the four basic colors: black, yellow, red, blue. A two-color page will be: black-white or black-red or black-blue. The SuperBowl is the final of American football in the U.S.A.

6) What are the 4 institutional communication techniques?
7) What are the 4 targets of institutional communication?

6) Sponsorship, patronage, sponsorship, patronage,
7) Financial circles, company personnel, clients, public authorities.

True or False

1) A furniture distributor placed posters adorned with adhesive labels in the metro that each passerby could take off:
2) An internet travel site organized a hoax by placing pop-ups (pop-up advertising) which announced the construction of a transatlantic tunnel between Paris and New York:

1) True, 2) True.

3) A brand of deodorant organized karate fights to promote its products in hypermarkets:

4) A car manufacturer distributed more than 25,000 false tickets offering brand gadgets:

5) A pepper-flavored drink used interactive posters. Each time a passer-by approached the billboard, the poster sneezed:

6) 85% of French people listen to the radio at least once a day:

7) The return rate of a highly targeted email can reach 20%:

8) The expression Spam comes from an English ham brand:

9) During advertisements on television or on the radio, the volume increases by 20%:

10) The most expensive advertising price is the niche 7:50 / 8 pm just before the television news:

3) True, 4) True, 5) True, 6) True, 7) False, 1%, 8) True, 9) True, 10) True.

Did you know it?

11) What do cinema advertising investments represent?
12) How many cinema tickets are sold in France in a year?
13) What are these oldest television programs in France:
.57 years, the 5 minutes most watched each day by the French, .55 years, the big loop most followed each

summer, .54 years, information on the television, .47 years old, every Sunday.

14) The 3 main advertisers in the cinema in France?

11) 1%, 12) 200 million/year, 13) Weather, Tour de France, 8 p.m. news, sports broadcast. 14) Retailers, Car manufacturers, Confectionery.

1) The "Lumière" brothers created cinema in: 1890, 1892, 1895,

2) The first sound film "The Jazz Singer" dates from: 1927, 1929, 1932,

3) The first blockbuster "Gone with the wind" is presented in: 1936, 1938, 1939,

4) The first Dolby sound film "Orange Mechanics" was made in: 1970, 1972, 1971,

5) The first 100% computer animation film was:

6) The VHS video recorder is essential in: 1975, 1978, 1977,

7) DVD players take half of the video market from: 2000, 2001, 2002,

8) The first all-digital film "Vidocq" dates from: 1999, 2000, 2001,

9) What does DVD mean?

10) A successful film is a blockbuster, what is the origin of this expression?

11) What does Wi-Fi mean?

1) 1895, 2) 1927, 3) 1939, 4) 1971, 5) Toy Story, 6) 1977, 7) 2001, 8) 2001, 9) Digital versatile disc, 10) Powerful bomb capable of exploding a block of houses, 11) Wireless Fidelity.

F/ Marketing MCQs

1) A brand :
a. Must be evocative, memorable, readable, adaptable, translatable,
b. Cannot be rented or sold,
c. Can be represented by a logo, an acronym, a word, a music,
d. May be misleading to the consumer.

2) An "umbrella" brand is:
a. Used in bad weather,
b. A reference mark for several product brands,
c. Often dependent on a signature brand (industrial holding company),
d. A retail brand.

3) The National Institute of Industrial Property (INPI):
a. Protects a brand for 10 years,
b. Protects a patent for 20 years,
c. Is a guarantee to protect against counterfeiting,
d. Allows you to protect a brand worldwide.

4) A company can use an existing brand:
a. Without any particular procedure,
b. If its sector of activity is different,
c. When negotiating with the owners,
d. By renting or buying this brand.

1) a. c., 2) b. c., 3) a. b., 4) b. c. d.

5) The packaging allows to:
a. Protect the products against external aggressions,
b. Communicate with the consumer,
c. Facilitate transport and handling,
d. Quickly place the products on the shelves.

6) Improving the quality of a product allows:
a. To multiply sales by three,
b. To eliminate competitors,
c. To improve the safety and modernity of a product,
d. To seduce the consumer and trigger the purchase.

7) A discontinuity product is:
a. An existing product that has been improved,
b. A product in the maturity phase,
c. A revolutionary and original product,
d. A product whose content has changed.

8) The BCG matrix means:
a. Better Consumer Guarantee,
b. Boston Community Graduate,
c. Boston Consulting Group,
d. Boston Consulting Great.

5) a. b. c. d., 6) c. d., 7) c., 8) c.

9) The BCG matrix allows:
a. To Analyze a product portfolio and their profitability,
b. To Calculate the break-even point,
c. To plan the products to be promoted and developed,
d. To know the company's bottom line.

10) The BCG matrix includes 4 types of products:
a. Leading, regulating, profitable and declining products,
b. Dilemmas, dead weights, stars and cash cows,
c. Star products, question mark, cash cows and dogs,
d. Products in research, launch, maturity and decline.

11) The SWOT matrix allows:
a. To prepare a super, wonderful, original and top strategy,
b. To know the strengths, weaknesses, opportunities and threats,
c. Analyze the audience of a press support,
d. Determine strengths, weaknesses, opportunities and threats.

12) The Porter's diagram allows:
a. To analyze threats from new entrants,
b. To anticipate substitution products,
c. To know the intensity of competition,
d. To prepare an e.mailing campaign.

9) a. c., 10) b. c., 11) b. d., 12) a. b. c.

13) The PESTEL scheme allows:
a. To know the evolution of the market in the short term,
b. To analyze the Problems, Equations and Elementary Works,
c. Create a PERT network,
d. Among others, to analyze the Political, Economic and Sociological aspects of a market.

14) The Value Analysis allows:
a. To know the utility value and the rarity value of a product,
b. To measure the esteem and exchange value of a commodity,
c. To know the use value of a product or service,
d. To measure the exchange rate of a currency.

15) The concept of Low Cost was invented:
a. By low-cost airlines,
b. By distributors at low prices,
c. By companies manufacturing in China,
d. By management controllers.

16) A communication target:
a. Incorporates potential buyers,
b. Incorporates potential buyers plus communication relays,
c. Incorporates real and potential consumers,
d. Incorporates relative and absolute consumers.

13) d., 14) a. b. c., 15) b. hard discounter, 16) b.

G/ Case Studies

These cases are prepared in pairs or in teams. An oral presentation is made using a computer and conventional software.

A / "Fast Food" case study:
According to you and based on your research on the internet:
1 / Why did "Fast Food" leave the French market in 1997?
2 / What is the "Fast Food" strategy at the international level, particularly in Europe and especially in France?
3 / What is your opinion on the new strategy adopted by "Fast Food" in France?
4 / If you were strategy consultants for "Fast Food", what would be your 5 commercial recommendations to develop in France and adapt to the French consumer?
5 / In order to create a Buzz on social networks, you must create a comparative and satirical advertising sketch promoting "Fast Food 1" against "Fast Food 2". This sketch is illustrated by a slideshow.

B / "Air Plane" case study:
1 / Explain and present the positioning of the "Air Plane" Group in a SWOT matrix and a Porter diagram,
2 / Explain "Air Plane's" international marketing strategy - what are the sales techniques for "Air Plane" salespeople?
3 / Offer two advertising slogans for "Air Plane" for export.

4 / Prepare an advertising scenario for a one-minute TV spot for "Air Plane" aircraft XXX which connects Paris to New York daily - all members of each team present this spot at the end of the session. The context, the scenario and the dialogues of the spot are written.

C / "DelivExpress" case study:

1 / Explain the positioning of the "DEX" Group in an ANSOFF matrix and explain the business environment in a PESTEL scheme.

2 / Explain "DEX's" international marketing strategy, particularly in Europe. How could "DEX's" competitors react to resist this commercial offensive?

3 / Offer two advertising slogans for "DEX" in English and three new services intended for French customers of "DEX".

4 / Prepare a slideshow of 5 visuals (photos, diagrams, etc.) including advertising information and a commercial slogan. This slideshow will be broadcast by MMS on the smartphones of "DEX" loyal customers.

D / "HyperMarket" case study:

Marketing assistant in the company "Shopping-Line", you must advise HyperMarket for a new project. Interested in the principle of automatic dispensers "HyperMarket" wishes to create an extra-large distributor of food products. Before entering the French market,

"HyperMarket" wishes to carry out a "market test" in England.

1 / Recall the current structure of local trade in England.

2 / What are the characteristics of the attitudes and behaviors of English businessmen.

3 / After choosing a name for this new distributor and an advertising slogan affixed to these machines, you must create a 3D model of this project (Maximum: 20 cm wide, 15 cm deep, 20 cm high) in paper / cardboard or on computer.

4 / In order to promote this distributor, a poster will be placed on the boxes of YYY hypermarkets - create this poster (A4 format) in paper / cardboard or on a computer.

5 / A 2-minute advertising spot will be broadcast in cinemas in London and its region. Write a script and prepare an advertising video for your new vending machine.

Sales Simulations

.Teamwork,

.Using the website of "Amusement Park ":
- Prepare an argument list with 6 objections and 6 reasoned answers for the "Amusement Park" for a specific business convention organised by "PubliStar" (advertising agency in France).
- Prepare a sales record (one page) including the 10 strengths of "Amusement Park Business Solutions" in order of interest for the customer,
- Prepare a sales simulation with the following themes to be developed:

1 / As a Sales Manager of "Amusement Park Business Solutions", you must face a very demanding prospect with a high potential turnover: "PubliStar" a worldwide advertising agency based in Paris.

This company wants to organize a convention for all its European and American subsidiaries in the Amusement Park. The representatives of this agency are particularly arrogant and require very stringent conditions from "Amusement Park Business Solutions"

Several clashes took place at the beginning of the interview, especially regarding the price. Given the tense situation, prepare a sales simulation lasting 15 minutes including a win-win agreement at the end of the simulation. All the members of each team attend the simulation during the oral presentation (at least 2 buyers and 2 sellers).

2 / As a Sales Managers at "World Luxury Services", you receive very wealthy potential customers from Switzerland. These services are very complex to organize (imagine any kind of service in your sales scenario). Very disappointed by a previous experience with WLS, these prospects require tough conditions and excellent services. The objective of WLS will be to satisfy even the strangest and special requirements of these clients.

Prepare a sales simulation lasting 15 minutes including a win-win agreement at the end of the simulation. All the members of each team attend the simulation during the oral presentation (at least two buyers and two sellers).

3 / "Coffee Star" asks you to convince business leaders of your business area to buy a breakfast package for their executives. You must present to the class a 3-minute speech about this new service. You may look like a politician or an artist speaking enthusiastically to a crowd of admirers.

1 / US Bank management case study:

New banking network in the United States, the "US Bank" offers a new mode of banking distribution with a very innovative management. Interested in the French market, "US Bank" executives would like to open branches in major French cities.

1 / What is your opinion on the methods of staff training and management of the "US Bank"?

2 / What do you think of the "Wow Program"?

3 / Do you think that the management principles of the "US Bank" could be applied in France?

4 / What types of encouragement and motivation system would you offer to stimulate future French managers?

5 / In order to participate in social or humanitarian programs, what could the "US Bank" offer in France?

2 / Martin and Martin management case study:

As consultants of "PCG" (Paris Consulting Group), you have been contacted by the M2 group. They want to use the latest management methods in a new subsidiary in Europe. They ask you to come up with new ideas and imagine the perfect business.

Based on your personal knowledge and even your management dreams, what would be your recommendations for the following points:

. Location of the business: Country, city, district,. Types and design of offices (plan, layout, materials, equipment),

. Hierarchical links,
. Types of relations between managers and subordinates,
. Leadership style,
. Remuneration and reward system,
. Types of relations with unions, . Stress management in the company .

In order to recruit successful managers, you must also prepare a recruitment advertisement which will be broadcast on the news channels continuously. Write a 30-second scenario (context, dialogue, staging), then play the commercial in front of the class.

H/ Economic Culture

True or False

1) 1% of the richest Americans shared last year 93% of the income created:
2) This wealthy 1% has more than a third of the national wealth:
3) While the income of 99% of Americans has increased only by 15% in the last thirty years, this 1% has increased theirs by 150%:
4) The 400 richest taxpayers share 5% of the dividends of the USA:
5) Wealth of the 3 richest men of the USA represents more than 150 billion dollars, that is to say the public deficit of France each year:

1) True, 2) True, 3) True, 4) True, 5) True.

6) An American billionaire has proposed to buy the Louvre museum in order to reduce the debt of the French State:
7) The turnover of the largest American company is equivalent to the GDP of France:
8) An American CEO earns on average more than 300 times the salary of a basic employee:

6) False, 7) False, Belgium, 8) True.

Did you know it?

- What are the unemployment rates in the following countries: Japan, Netherlands, Germany, Sweden, United Kingdom, United States, Italy, France, Euro zone, Greece, Spain.

(2019 figures):
Japan 2.4%, Netherlands 3.3%, Germany 3.1%, Sweden 6.3%, United Kingdom 3.7%, United States 3.5%, Italy 9.9%, France 8.6%, Euro Zone 6.3%, Greece 18.1%, Spain 13.6%.

9) Which country of the European Union whose annual number of births has halved since 1965 will have lost a fifth of its inhabitants in 2060:
10) Which European country has 1.3 million vacancies due to a workforce shortage:
11) What is the fertility rate in Germany:
12) There are 7.5 billion human beings, 3 billion internet users and 4 billion mobile phone users on the planet:
13) In European Union, VAT Fraud amounts to 120 billion euros, or 17% of the amount collected:
14) In 2030, out of 8 billion inhabitants, 6 billion will live in the countryside:
15) China represents 49% of the world production of crude steel, for 15% in 1999:
16) Total average value of the players on the ground for a match of first division in Spain:

9) Germany, 10) Germany, 11) 1.5 children per woman, 12) True, 13) True, 14) False, in cities, 15) True, 16) $ 1.3 billion.

17) In the next twenty years, the number of passengers on planes will be halved:
18) 90% of world financial exchanges are made in dollars:
19) In the Top 20 international universities, 18 are American:
20) The main American search engine holds 90% of the world market share:
21) The American defense budget amounts to 495 billion dollars:

17) False, multiplied by two, 18) True, 19) True, 20) True, 21) True.

1) Developed countries and prosperous areas of developing countries represent less than 20% of the world population:
2) German luxury car manufacturers sell more vehicles in China than in Germany:
3) In Bangladesh, some cellphones are rented for each call:
4) Some producers of hygiene products use advertising trucks in India to show promotional films for brushing teeth:
5) In Mexico and Chile, residences are built with containers maritime transport:

6) The Nova was a failure in South America because this brand locally meant "Does not work":

1) True, 2) True, 3) True, 4) True, 5) True, 6) True.

7) The MR2 was a failure in France because of the meaning of the brand:
8) In Egypt, cheese servings are sold individually in local grocery stores, each serving is worth a few cents:

7) True, 8) True.

9) The major aircraft manufacturers had to create Joint Ventures with local companies in order to set up in China:
10) To sell its vehicles in Brazil, European manufacturers must use Flex-Fuel engines in order to use local bio fuel based on sugar cane:
11) Some Brazilian airlines fly with bio fuels:

9) True, 10) True, 11) False.

12) Why an advertisement with a white clown would not be recommended in Japan:
13) The producers of cleaning products sold very little wax for floors in Japan because,
- the brown color of the product brings bad luck,
- the product contains dangerous chemicals,
- Japanese people do not wear shoes at home or polish their floors.

12) Because white makeup evokes death.

13) Japanese people do not wear shoes at home and do not polish their floors.

14) The producers of industrial dishes have not managed to sell pastry preparations in Japan because,
- the Japanese do not eat pastry,
- only 3% of Japanese households are equipped with an oven,
- the Japanese do not make pastry.

15) Fast food restaurants offer:
.rice and Broccoli in Hong Kong / rye bread in Finland / moose in Canada.

14) only 3% of Japanese households have an oven,
15) rice and Broccoli in Hong Kong / rye bread in Finland /

16) On average, an apartment in central London rents for 10,000 euros per month for a 3-room apartment and 30,000 euros per month for a house:

17) An apartment in London is 150% more expensive than in Paris:

18) In terms of property prices, New York is the most expensive city in the world:

19) The 67 wealthiest people in the world have as much wealth as the poorest half of the world's population:

16) True, 17) True, 18) False, London. 19) True.

1) Sold around 659 € in France, what is the cost of manufacturing a smartphone in China: 24 € - 131 € - 436 €,

2) What is the average amount of expenses of a Chinese tourist in Paris per day and per brand, 400 € - 700 € - 1300 €,

3) Who is the main tourist clientele of Parisian cabarets: Japanese tourists - American tourists - Chinese tourists,

4) Chinese tourists in Paris spend € 650 million - € 120 million per year - 210 million €,

5) Chinese tourists represent 25% of the turnover of Parisian department stores - 5% - 90%, 6) Some tour operators sometimes sold entry tickets to Notre-Dame de Paris while access was free:

7) 80% of the budget of a Chinese tourist in Paris is devoted to luxury brands:

1) € 131, 2) € 1,300, 3) Chinese tourists, 4) € 650 million, 5) 25%, 6) True, 7) True.

8) Tourists visiting Paris sometimes sleep in tour operator buses in order to save on the hotel budget:

9) In front of certain Chinese restaurants in Paris, Duty Free shops are sometimes set up to attract this clientele after meals:

10) In the tour program of certain tour operators, the visit to the Louvre is often completed in an hour - the Eiffel Tower is simply photographed:

11) What was the distribution of the major world powers during the following periods:
.1870: France - United Kingdom - Germany
.1973: Germany - USA - Japan

.2010: China - USA - Japan
.2030 (forecast): India - China - USA
12) What is the decreasing ranking of the richest countries in GDP per capita in thousands of dollars: Switzerland - Netherlands - Luxembourg - Norway - Brunei - United States - Qatar - Singapore - United Arab Emirates - Hong Kong.

8) False, 9) True, 10) True,
11) .1870: France (3) - United Kingdom (1) - Germany (2). 1973: Germany (3) - USA (1) - Japan (2). 2010: China (2) - USA (1) - Japan (3). 2030 (forecast) : India (3) - China (1) - USA (2)
12) Switzerland (9) - Netherlands (10) - Luxembourg (2) - Norway (4) - Brunei (5) - United States (7) - Qatar (1) - Singapore (3) - United Arab Emirates (6) - Hong-Kong (8).

13) One in 10 European babies would be conceived in a Swedish brand bed:
14) What is the new diversification of furniture stores: wooden kit cars - wooden planes in kit - wooden houses in kit,

15) The catalog of a Swedish furniture dealer is written in, 29 languages - 12 languages - 19 languages,

16) Their catalog is printed at, 35 million copies - 198 million - 110 million,

17) Their catalog is the second publication in the world in number of copies after: the Directory - the Bible - the Michelin Guide,

18) In Hong-Kong, a fast food offers a new service: the "Fast Wedding", the future spouses get married in the restaurant and organize the wedding meal there:

19) In some furniture stores in China, it is possible to see consumers who take their nap in an exhibition bed or who settle in the sofas to play with their smartphone:

13) True, 14) Wooden houses in kit form, 15) 29 languages, 16) 198 million, 17) the Bible, 18) True, 19) True,

20) Their cafeteria is often occupied by retirees who meet there to look for a soul mate and have a coffee:

21) A supermarket in Beijing had to install the following information panels, "The games department and toys is not a daycare center, children cannot be left there by their parents ":

20) True, 21) True.

22) In order to ride the "RetailTainment" trend, supermarkets have planned to add attractions at their points of sale, clown shows, giant slides, sumo fights:

23) Certain banner advertising campaigns for chocolate bars are scheduled to appear on websites at snack time:

24) The cost of using disposable cleaning wipes is fifteen times higher for the consumer than the cost of using traditional products:

25) Perfume brands adapt their advertising according to two areas, the Middle East (mannequins less undressed and hair covered) and the rest of the world:

22) False, 23) True, 24) True, 25) True.

26) In the animal feed market, certain products are intended for consumers whose cat is considered a lover's substitute and others for whom the cat is a friendly animal:

27) In Europe, Diet sodas have been replaced by "Light" because the term "Diet" evokes severe regimes:

28) In France, American Fast Foods are multiplying the locations on motorway areas:

29) What is the classification of tax havens in descending order of bank deposits , in billions of dollars, Switzerland - Luxembourg - Belgium - Hong-Kong - Cayman Islands - Singapore - Jersey, 30) What is the amount of financial wealth held by households in tax havens: 2,000 billion euros - 5,000 - 1,200

26) True, 27) True, 28) True, 29) Switzerland (5) - Luxembourg (4) - Belgium (7) - Hong-Kong (1) - Cayman Islands (2) - Singapore (3) - Jersey (6), 30) 5,000.

31) If these fortunes were taxed by their respective States, they would bring in: 120 billion euros each year - 30 – 46

31) 120 billion euros each year - 30 - 46.

32) Last year, the tax departments of the various western countries recovered in certain tax havens (Switzerland, Luxembourg, etc.), 200 million euros - 830 million - 14 billion,
33) Which country has 60% of its sports champions living in Switzerland for tax reasons:
34) Which country of the European Union has the highest VAT rate:
35) Which European country do the wealthiest residents (Shipowners and Clergy) pay no tax: 36) Which European port was bought in part by a Chinese bank:

32) 200 million euros, 33) France, 34) Hungary (27%), France (20%) , European average: 21%, lowest VAT rate (Luxembourg, 17%), 35) Greece, 36) The port of Piraeus in Athens in Greece.

◆◆◆

I/ International Marketing Calculations

A / BioTop wishes to participate in the Alimentaria tradefair in Barcelona in order to convince the central purchasing office of the Spanish Super Mercado hypermarkets.
Calculate the overall cost of this operation.
. Participants: 1 sales manager and 2 sales people,
. Registration for the Alimentaria fair*: € 299,
. Booth*: € 5900,
. Plane ticket: € 279 € (round trip Nantes-Barcelona on a low cost airline),
. Hotel: one night plus breakfast, € 49,
. Arrival on Monday April 1 at 11 am. and departure on Sunday April 7 at 9 am.
. Meals (unit cost, noon and evening): € 29 per meal,
. Taxi *: 119 €, . Tasting products *: € 1,860
. Bilingual hostess *: € 759
. Advertising brochures *: € 1,319
. Free buffet on the booth*: € 1,249

. * Global cost.

A / *Answers* :
. *Plane: 279 x 3 = € 837*
. *Hotel: 49 x 6 nights x 3 people = € 882*
. *Meals: 29 x 2 meals x 6 days x 3 people = € 1,044.*
Total: € 2,763.
Total operation: € 14,268 (2,763 + fixed costs).

All lump sum costs are paid at once for the entire commercial operation.

B / The MotosFrance dealer buys Hurley-Dujohnson bikes in the United States.

The FOB New York price has been set at 29,000 US dollars. Shipping from New York to the port of Le Havre costs $ 2,900. The American forwarder is paid $ 790.

The customs duties applicable to imports into the European Union are 15% of the commercial value of the goods. The applicable VAT on imports is 20%. 1 USD = 0.73 €.

How much will MotosFrance have to pay to market these American motorcycles in France?

B / *Answers :*

. FOB, free on board.

The seller pays the shipping costs to the port of New York. The risk of transport is transferred to the buyer as soon as the container is placed on the ship from the port of New York.

.Delivery to the port of Le Havre: 29,000 + 2,900 + 790 = 32,690 USD.

32690 USD x 0.73 = € 23863.7.   23863.7 x 1.15 (import customs duties) = € 27,443.25.

27443.25 x 1.2 (import VAT) = € 32,931.9.

The total amount payable by the French importer is approximately € 32,932.

VAT is still paid by the importer. The exporter is exempt from VAT.

◆◆◆

C / A commercial attaché for the company SuperGreen is trying to prospect the Benelux market (Belgium, Netherlands, Luxembourg) in order to market dishes prepared without pesticides. His fixed compensation is € 1,000 per month.

He receives a mileage reimbursement of € 0.5 per kilometer and travels around 4,000 km per month. One week he visits clients from his region in France, one week he visits clients in the Benelux.

For his trips to the Benelux, he receives a reimbursement of € 50 per hotel night. His restaurant expenses are not reimbursed. SuperGreen must pay 50% of employer charges on the wages paid. The commercial attaché makes his visits from Monday afternoon to Friday morning inclusive.

He meets an average of 3 customers per half-day and signs around 3 orders for 4 visits. He is on internship for one week per year and goes on paid vacations for 5 weeks per year.

1 / Calculate the cost of a visit to this commercial attaché.
2 / What is the average amount of an order to reach the breakeven point? (Unit margin: 8%).

C / *Answers* :

1/ Cost of a visit: .Fixed wage: 1,000 x 1.5 (employer contributions) x 12 months = 18,000.

Car costs: 0.5 x 4000 x 10.5 months (12 months - 6 weeks away) = 21,000.

Hotel costs: 50 x 4 nights = 200 x 2 weeks per month x 10.5 months = 4200.

Total: € 43,200. Number of visits: 3 customers x 8 half days x 4 weeks x 10.5 months = 1,008 visits, € 43,200 / 1,008 visits = € 42.85 per visit.

2 / Break even point: A visit costs € 42.85, an order costs € 57.13 (42.85 x 4/3).
Fixed charges 57.13 / 0.08 unit margin = € 714.12.
. The break-even point is around € 714.5 per order.

D / A French soda maker wants to sell its FrenchCola in the United States. The American distributor Fresco orders 2 pallets to test this new drink. A palette includes 40 cases of sodas. Each soda signed by a contemporary artist is sold for € 7 per unit.

A 20kg case contains 12 bottles. One bottle contains 0.75 liters of soda.

Packaging costs: a pallet costs € 90, a case € 12 and a bottle € 1.4.

Transport costs: between 1 and 2 tonnes, € 622 per tonne; between 2 and 3 tonnes, € 474 per tonne.

Margin rate on the purchase cost of the distributor Fresco: 35%.

VAT in the United States for soft drinks: 15%.

Import duties in the United States: $ 33.49 per hectoliter for production less than 1000 hectoliters.

Exchange rate: $ 1 = € 0.95. One hectoliter = 100 liters.
What will be the amount payable by the American distributor and the unit public price in the United States?

D/ Answers :

.Order amount: 2 pallets of 40 cases (12 bottles per case), 2 x 40 x 12 = 960 bottles x € 7 =
€ 6,720.
Packaging costs: 2 pallets x € 90 + 80 cases x € 12 + 960 bottles x € 1.4 = € 2,484.
Total weight: 80 cases x 20 kg = 1,600 kg (1.6 tonnes).
Paying rule for: 2 tonnes x € 474 <1.6 tonnes x € 622.
In a transport scale, it is possible to find cheaper in the immediately higher price range. The shipper can therefore transport more goods at a lower price. The "pay for" rule is always to the advantage of the shipper. FrenchCola will retain 2 tonnes at € 474 = € 948.
. Amount to be paid by the American distributor: 6720 + 2484 + 948 = € 10,152.
. Exchange rate: € 10,152 = $ 10,686.31 (10,152 / 0.95).
. Amount of resale in the United States: 10,686.31 x 1.35 (margin on purchase cost) =
$ 14,426.52.
Customs duties: $ 33.49 x 7.2 hl (960 bottles x 0.75 liter = 720 liters or 7.2 hectolitre) =
$ 241.13.
Import VAT: 14,426.52 + 241.13 = 14,667.6 x 1.15 = $ 16,867.7 (Total import cost, VAT is paid by the importer).
. Unit price of a bottle of soda in the United States: 16,867.7 / 960 = $ 17.57.

◆◆◆

E / The French arborist StarFruits concluded a sale of 5,400 kg of pears with a Norwegian importer from Oslo Scandinavian Ltd.
The h.t price per kilo of pears from StarFruits is € 0.91.
Transport by truck and insurance: € 0.24 per kg.
Customs duties: € 0.2 per kg. 2% discount for all orders paid in cash. The amount to pay is in US dollars. € 1 = $ 1.2. Sale in DDP Oslo.
What is the amount payable by the Norwegian importer who will pay in cash?

E / *Answers* :

.DDP: *Delivery Duty Paid, the seller must pay the transport costs to the destination of the foreign buyer. He assumes the risks of transport to the point determined with the customer in the country of arrival.*
. Starting price: 0.91 x 5,400 kg = € 4,914.
Discount 2%: 4914 - 2% = € 4,815.72 (Net price).
Transport / Insurance: € 0.24 x 5,400 kg = € 1,296.
Import customs duties: € 0.2 x 5,400 kg = € 1,080.
Amount to pay in €: 7,191.72 €.
Amount to pay in $: 7,191.72 x 1.2 = $ 8,630.06.
h.t: (VAT) tax excluded.

J/ International Negotiation

True or False

1) To have a monochronic behavior means that time is considered linear - you do only one thing at a time - the communication is direct, organized and detailed:

2) The Scandinavians are more monochronic:

3) The Mediterranean countries are monochronic:

4) Spain and Italy often have a polychronic behavior – time is multidimensional:

5) The notion of uncertainty varies between countries - Muslim countries are rather fatalistic, Westerners are more anxious about an uncertain future:

6) At a first business contact, the Swedes use the first name:

7) In South America, only leaders have the power to negotiate:

8) In Japan, you have to remove your shoes in public places, especially in a supermarket:

9) In Japan, for a business relationship, you do not shake hands and you avoid to be too close to your customer:

10) In the United States, it is common to offer gifts to loyal customers:

11) In Asia, business gifts are common and recommended

12) In Sweden, the meetings always start late:

13) In Mexico or Saudi Arabia, to arrive on time seems very surprising: 14) In the UK, a verbal agreement is very common:

1) True, 2) True, 3) False, 4) True, 5) True, 6) True, 7) True, 8) False, 9) True, 10) False, 11) True, 12) False, 13) True, 14) True.

Which negotiator is used to these behavior and attitudes: . French Negotiatior – English Negotiator – Spanish Negotiator – German Negotiator

1) Clear and strong, few concessions, no relationship of friendship, only the result counts, logical presentation, structured, supported by figures, facts and references:

2) Sense of pride and honor, modesty more than assertiveness, adept at haggling, interpersonal relationship appreciated, few group works:

3) Reserve and self control, not expressing emotions, discretion on the personal and private life, taste for humor and self-deprecation, predominance of the oral over the written, a follower of customary law:

4) Written documents are a priority with polite and complex expressions, ignorance of foreign languages, indirect communication, often intransigent, follower of the debates and arguments:

1) German, 2) Spanish, 3) English, 4) French.

-Which country uses the following currencies:
Rand, Riyal, Yuan, Forint, Rupee, Yen, Shequel, Bath, Dong, Peso, Won.

Thailand (Bath) Mexico (Peso) Japan (Yen) Israel (Shequel) Vietnam (Dong) South Korea (Won) India (Rupee) South Africa (Rand), Saudi-Arabia (Riyal), China (Yuan), Hungary (Forint).

-In Which cities can you use these airports:
CDG, JFK, La Guardia, Heathrow, Newark, Stansted, Gatwick, O'Hare, Mirabel, Schiphol, Logan, Bora Bora, Fiumicino, Fortworth:

CDG : Paris, JFK : New York, La Guardia : New York, Heathrow : London, Newark : New York, Stansted : London, Gatwick : London, O'Hare : Chicago, Mirabel : Montreal, Schiphol : Amsterdam, Logan : Boston, Bora Bora : Papeete, Fiumicino : Roma, Fortworth : Dallas.

◆◆◆

-From Paris, how long does it take to fly to these cities: Los Angeles, Papeete, Vancouver, Boston, Grenoble, Noumea ?
17h25, 25 h, 10 h30, 27 h, 6 h52, 0 h50 ?

Los Angeles (10h30), Papeete (25h), Vancouver (17h25), Boston (6h52), Grenoble (0h50), Noumea (27h).

-To which countries do these Airlines belong ? Aeroflot, Lufthansa, Federal Express, KLM, Varig, Olympic Airways, El Al, . Iberia, Finnair, Qantas, Avianca, Emirates, Air Perhaps, Continental Airlines.

Aeroflot(Russia), Lufthansa(Germany), Federal Express(USA), KLM (France), Varig(Brésil), Olympic Airways(Grèce), El Al(Israël), Iberia(U.K), Finnair(Finland), Qantas(Australia), Avianca(Colombia), Emirates(UAE), Air Perhaps, Continental Airlines(USA).

K/ Geography Quiz

Please find the following American States:

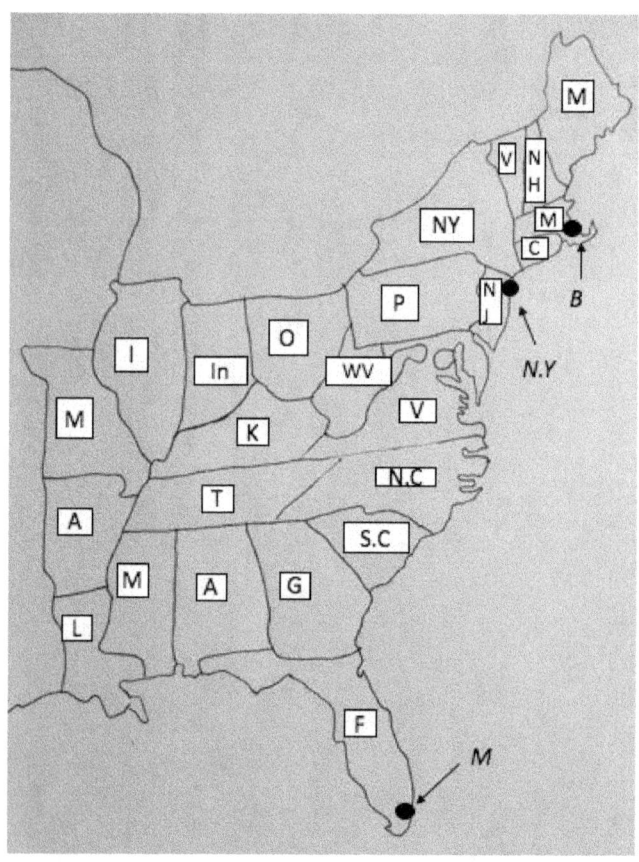

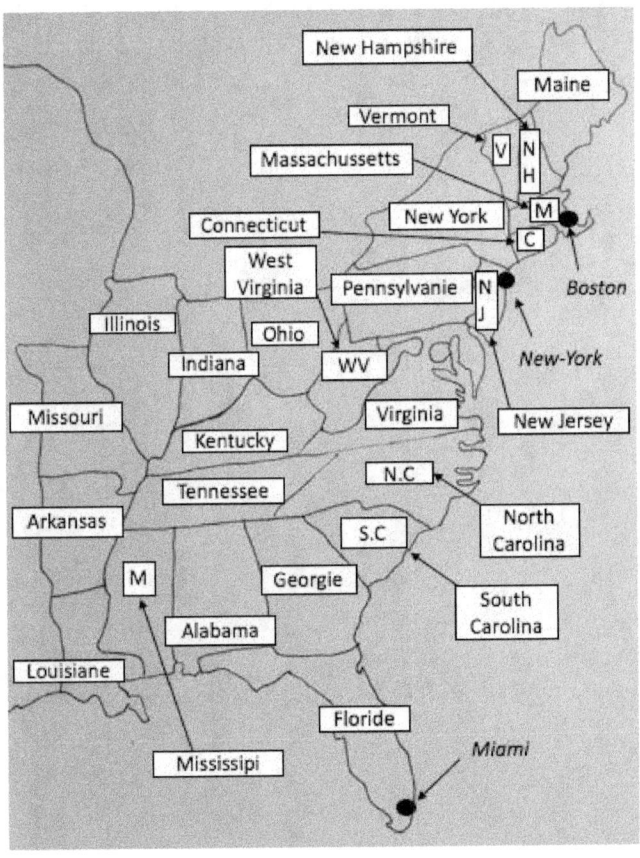

.Floride: Florida, Géorgie: Georgia, Pennsylvanie: Pennsylvania.

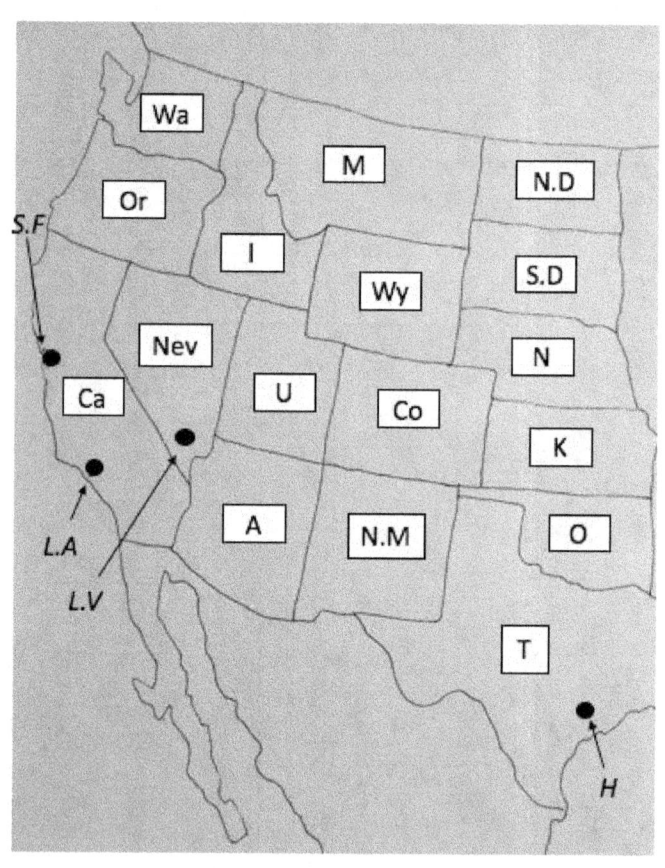

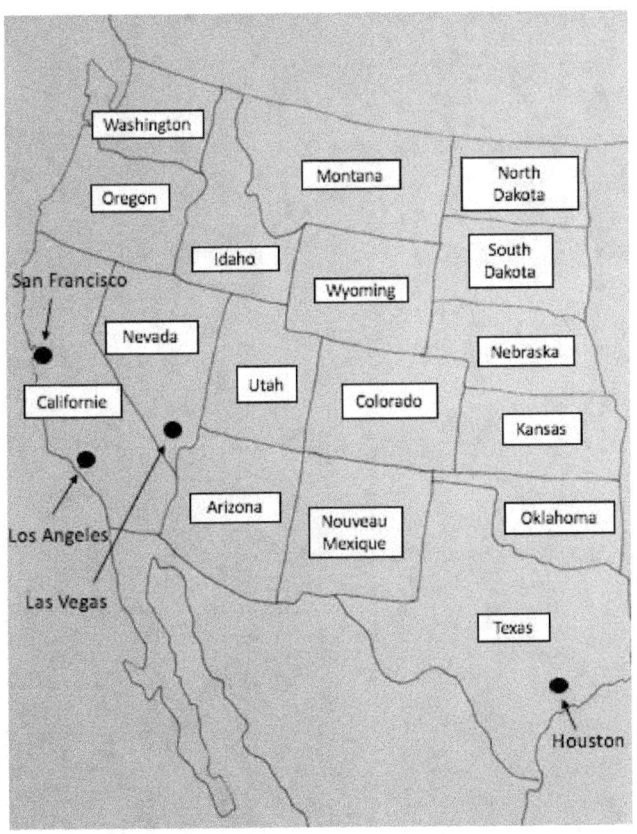

.Nouveau Mexique: New Mexico,
Californie: California.

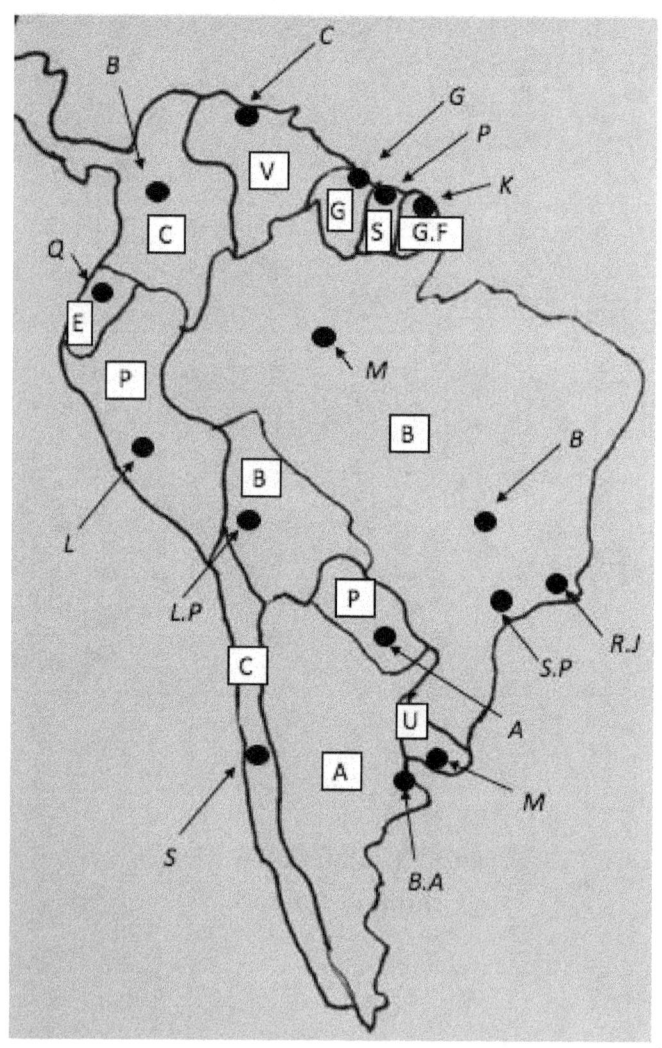

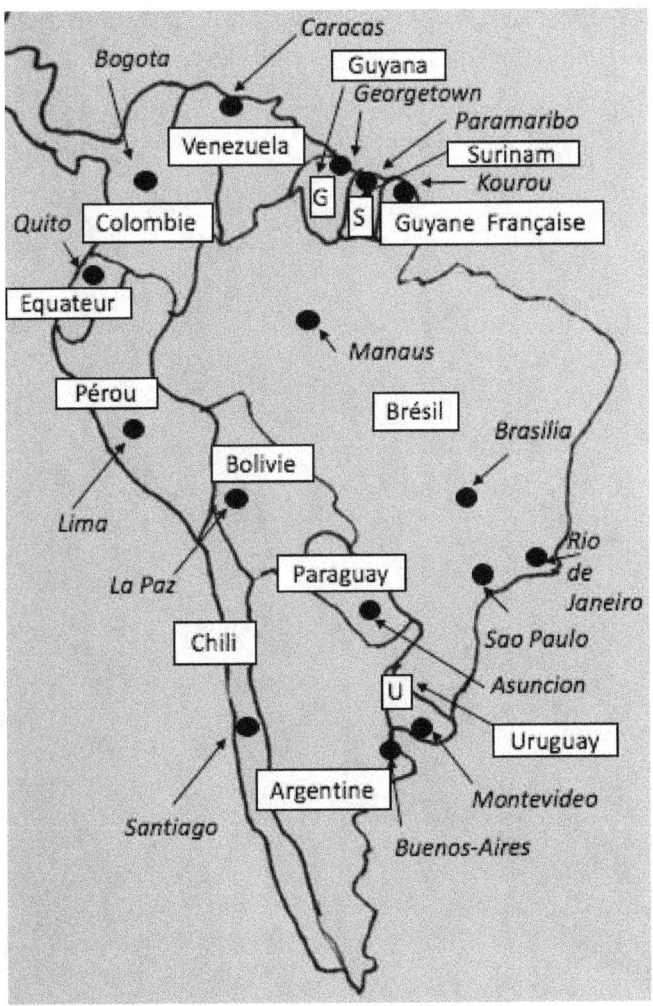

From the same author

La Vie Epatante de l'Agent Secret Duchemin – Tome 1
Il Faut Sauver l'Agent Secret Duchemin – Tome 2
Agent Secret Duchemin – Mission Lune – Tome 3
Au Temps en Emporte l'Agent Duchemin – Tome 4
Le Fabuleux Destin de l'Agent Duchemin – Tome 5
Agent Secret Duchemin-En Avant Mars – Tome 6
Agent Secret Duchemin – A Mars Forcée – Tome 7
Agent Secret Duchemin - Un Héros Français -Tome 8
Agent Secret Duchemin-Opération Rédemption-Tome 9

L'Effarante Aventure de Brian Tabernak – Tome 1
L'Incroyable Attaque de l'agent Tabernak - Tome 2
La Terrible Traque de l'Equipe Tabernak – Tome 3
L'Equipe Tabernak Contre-Attaque – Tome 4
Des Agents pas très Secrets – Opération Esturgeon
Des Agents pas très Secrets – Mission Caméléon
Des Agents pas très Secrets - Maudite Météorite

Constantin Dumoulin – Panique sous les Tropiques
Constantin Dumoulin – Branle-Bas de Combat aux USA
Constantin Dumoulin – Secret Fatal au Lac Baïkal
Robin Dubois – Sans Froid ni Loi – Tome 1
Robin Dubois – Espion malgré moi – Tome 2

The Exciting Life of Secret Agent Duchemin – Volume 1
The Amazing Adventure of Brian Tabernak – Volume 1
The Incredible Attack of Agent Tabernak – Volume 2

Quiz de Marketing-Tome 1
Quiz de Marketing-Tome 2
Quiz de Marketing International
Quiz de Management Commercial
Marketing Quiz
Marketing Calculations

www.ingramcontent.com/pod-product-compliance
Lightning Source LLC
Chambersburg PA
CBHW070808220526
45466CB00002B/592